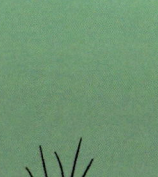

Good News! The Gospel Story for Kids
Copyright © 2024 Sarah Thomas

All rights reserved.

No part of this publication may be reproduced in a retrieval system, or transmitted in any form or by any means—electronic, mechanical, photocopying, recording, or otherwise—without the prior written permission of the publisher.

The Holy Bible, English Standard Version® (ESV®) Copyright © 2001 by Crossway, a publishing ministry of Good News Publishers. All rights reserved. ESV Text Edition: 2016.

This manuscript has undergone viable editorial work and proofreading, yet human limitations may have resulted in minor grammatical or syntax-related errors remaining in the finished book. The understanding of the reader is requested in these cases. While precaution has been taken in the preparation of this book, the publisher and author assume no responsibility for errors or omissions, or for damages resulting from the use of the information contained herein.

This book is set in the typeface Neuton designed by Brian Zick.

Storybooks by Sarah

Hardcover ISBN: 978-1-955546-61-4
Paperback ISBN: 978-1-955546-62-1

A Publication of *Tall Pine Books*
119 E Center Street, Suite B4A | Warsaw, Indiana 46580
www.tallpinebooks.com

| 1 24 24 20 16 02 |

Published in the United States of America

GOOD NEWS!

The Gospel Story For Kids

WRITTEN AND ILLUSTRATED BY
Sarah Thomas

God made the heavens and the earth.

He formed the land and sea.

Now, the snake was very crafty,
And he made an evil plan,

To separate the friendship,
That God had made with man.

When the snake lied to the people,
They turned from God and sinned.

Now we can live forever with Him,
Free from sickness, sin, and shame.

That's the good news of the Gospel,
Brought to you in Jesus' name!

The Good News is amazing,
But there's more great news to cover!

God sent another gift to us,
For each one to discover!

He sent his Holy Spirit
To be your helper and your guide.

He is always with you,
He lives on the inside!

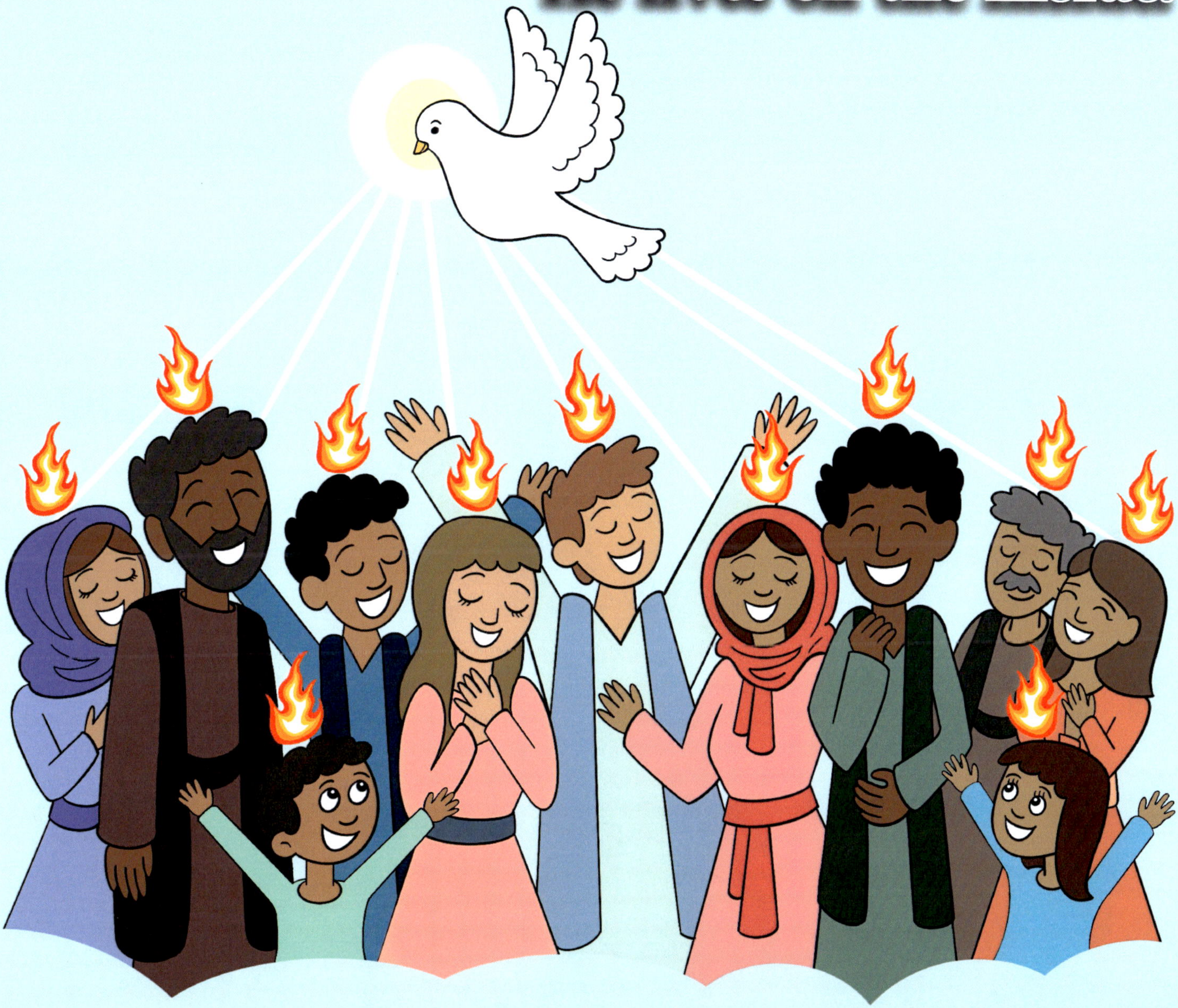

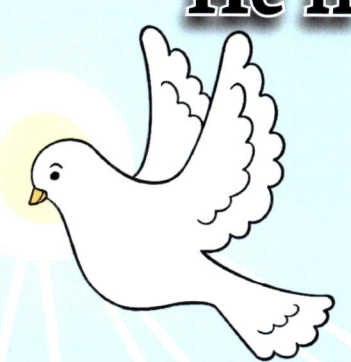

There's so much good in store for us,
In all that He has planned.

If you want to join God's family,
Then pray this prayer with me.

You'll belong to Jesus,
Forever His, you'll be!

God, please forgive me,

I receive Jesus Christ, Your Son.

I confess that He's my Lord!

Thank You, for all You've done!

I receive your Holy Spirit.

Come and make Your home in me.

Help me to follow Jesus, And become all I can be!

Amen.

A brand-new life in Jesus, Because you have believed!

Scripture References for the Good News book!

"For God so loved the world, that he gave his only Son, that whoever believes in him should not perish but have eternal life." (John 3:16)

"If you confess with your mouth that Jesus is Lord and believe in your heart that God raised him from the dead, you will be saved." (Romans 10:9)

"Jesus told him, 'I am the way, the truth, and the life. No one can come to the Father except through me'." (John 14:6)

"Then I will ask the Father to send you the Holy Spirit who will help you and always be with you." (John14:16)

"For I know what I have planned for you,' says the Lord. 'I have plans to prosper you, not to harm you. I have plans to give you a future filled with hope." (Jeremiah 29:11)

"In the same way, there is joy in the presence of God's angels when even one sinner repents." (Luke 15:10)